THE MINIATURE BOOK OF
Festive
Decorations

CRESCENT BOOKS
New York

© Salamander Books Ltd., 1990
129-137 York Way, London N7 9LG, United Kingdom

This 1990 edition published by Crescent Books, distributed
by Outlet Book Company, Inc., a Random House Company,
225 Park Avenue South, New York, New York 10003

ISBN 0-517-03724-6

Printed and bound in Belgium

87654321

CREDITS

PROJECTS BY: *Suzie Major*

EDITED BY: *Jilly Glassborow*

PHOTOGRAPHY BY: *Terry Dilliway*

DESIGN AND ARTWORK BY: *Pauline Bayne*

TYPESET BY: *SX Composing Ltd.*

COLOR SEPARATION BY: *Chroma Graphics (Overseas) Pte. Ltd.*

PRINTED IN BELGIUM BY: *Proost International Book Production,
Turnhout, Belgium*

Contents

Pretty Paper Chains

TRADITIONAL PAPER CHAINS
ARE ALWAYS A MUST AT
CHRISTMAS TIME

1 First cut two circles of cardboard and lots of circles of tissue paper, 4in (10cm) in diameter. Take about ten tissue paper circles and fold them together in four. Now make two curved cuts as shown, once from the single-folded edge, once from the double folds. Open out the circles. Glue the centre of the first circle to the middle of one cardboard circle.

2 Take a second tissue circle and glue it to the first at the top and bottom. Glue a third circle to the centre of the second circle. Continue in this way, remembering to glue alternate circles in the same place at the top and bottom. If you alter the positioning you will spoil the effect. Finally, glue the other cardboard circle to the last tissue circle.

3 Cut two 'flower-shaped' templates from cardboard and lots of tissue paper shapes. Dab glue on to every other petal of a tissue flower and stick a second flower on top. Dab glue on to those petals which weren't glued before and stick a third flower down. Build up the layers, gluing petals in alternate positions. Finally, stick a cardboard template to each end.

Highland Holly

DECK THE HALL WITH SPRIGS
OF HOLLY MADE FROM FELT
AND TARTAN RIBBON

1 First, make a holly pattern from paper and use this to cut out two pieces of green felt and one of wadding for every sprig. Place two felt pieces together, with the wadding in between, and pin in place. Now, with three strands of green embroidery thread, overstitch neatly all around the edges.

2 Thread your sewing machine with green cotton and stitch 'veins' on to each holly leaf – one down the centre and the rest sloping from the centre to the points. Next take four red wooden or plastic beads for each leaf and sew them in place, close to the inside edge, using six strands of red embroidery thread.

3 Measure out a length of tartan ribbon from which to hang the holly; the length will depend on the number of sprigs you are making. Now cut shorter lengths of ribbon – one per sprig – to make the bows. Tie the sprigs to the garland with the short lengths of ribbon, finishing off with a bow. Finally, cut a V-shape in the tails of the bows and hang your garland in place.

Santa Faces

ADD COLOUR AND CHEER TO
YOUR TREE WITH THESE
JOLLY SANTAS

1 Referring to the photograph, draw a pattern for the Santa faces and then cut out all the pieces in felt. Glue the main face piece to a piece of cardboard. When it is dry, cut around it.

2 All you have to do now is glue on all the other pieces. Fix the nose and cheeks first before applying the moustache, which goes on top.

3 Place a loop of thread under the circle on the top of the hat, to hang up the face. Finally, glue two dark sequins in place to represent the eyes.

Ping Pong Treats

DECORATE YOUR TREE WITH
BAUBLES MADE FROM
PING PONG BALLS

1 Take some ordinary ping pong balls and spear each one on to a fine knitting needle. Now paint the balls brown. After two or three coats, for a dark rich colour, finish off with a clear varnish to give the 'puddings' a lovely shine.

2 Take some Fimo modelling clay, the sort you bake in the oven, and roll it into a ball, the same size as the ping pong balls. Over this, mould a thick circle of white clay, to look like custard sauce. Bake this in the oven, then remove the topping from the clay ball straight away, and pop it on to a pudding, so that it fits as it cools down. Poke a hole in the top at this point.

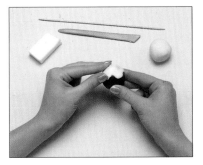

3 When the clay is cold, glue it to the pudding. Now take a large needle and double thread, knot the ends and thread it through the pudding from the bottom upwards. Trim off the ends, then finish each pudding by gluing on foil holly leaves and red bead berries.

Holiday Hoop-La!

TRANSFORM A HOOLA-HOOP
INTO A COLOURFUL
FESTIVE WREATH

1 To make this design you will need a plastic hoop; any size will do. Cut long strips of wadding and wind them around the hoop, holding the edges in place with sticky tape. We gave it two layers of medium-weight wadding.

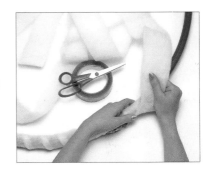

2 Next take some 3in (8cm) wide ribbon and wind it firmly around the hoop, in the opposite direction to the wadding. Make sure the wadding is entirely covered. Take a contrasting ribbon, about 2in (5cm) wide, and wrap it over the first ribbon, leaving equal spaces between the loops. Repeat with a third ribbon, 1in (2cm) wide.

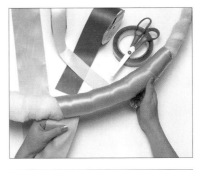

3 Make sure each ribbon starts and finishes in the same place so that all the joins are together. This will be the top of the hoop. Wind tinsel around the hoop, over the ribbons. Pin or staple a wide piece of ribbon in place to cover all the joins at the top. Tape a cluster of ribbons, tinsel, baubles and bells at the top and add a large bow to finish off.

Forest Foliage

DRESS UP THE SIDEBOARD
WITH THIS BRIGHT AND
CHEERY DESIGN

1 If you don't have woodland nearby, your florist should have small sections of bark for sale. Also buy a plastic candle holder. On to the bark, first put a large lump of green Plasticine (modelling clay), and on the top stick your candle holder.

2 Now take some plastic or silk fern and spray it gold. Break off pieces when it is dry, and stick them into the Plasticine. Also wire up strands of red paper ribbon, pine cones and red baubles and stick these in.

3 When the Plasticine is artistically concealed, pop a red candle in the holder, and set the arrangement on the sideboard. Put a mat under it, though, or it will scratch the surface.

Foliage Frame

THIS NATURAL DESIGN ADDS
A FESTIVE TOUCH TO A
MIRROR OR PICTURE

1 Make this design in separate sections, one to be horizontal, the other vertical. You need fake ivy, fern and other foliage, plus pine cones, gold baubles and gold curling gift wrap ribbon. Cut off the long stems and wire everything up as shown, using florist's wire.

2 For the top section, gradually lay pieces on top of one another, binding the wires and stems together with florist's tape as you go. The arrangement should be relatively long and narrow.

3 For the second section, use the same technique but make the arrangement fuller. Hold the two pieces as you would like them to sit on the frame, and wire them together. Bend the stem wires back so that they will slip over the frame and hold the arrangement in place.

Golden Platter

A TOUCH OF GOLD GIVES A
FESTIVE FRUIT PLATTER
EXTRA RICHNESS

1 Begin by spraying ivy, clementines, bay leaves and fir cones with gold paint. (If the fruit is to be eaten, make sure that the paint you are using is non-toxic.)

2 Place the ivy leaves around the edge of a plain oval platter. The flatter the plate, the better, for this will allow the ivy leaves to hang over the edge.

3 Arrange the clementines on the platter, surround them with dates and nuts, and place a bunch of shiny black grapes on top. Add the gold leaves and fir cones for a luxurious finishing touch.

23

Ribbons and Curls

A PROFUSION OF FLOWERS
AND BOWS MAKES A
FUN CENTREPIECE

1 Our design is pink and white, but you should choose whatever colours match your décor. First of all you will need a cake tin. Cover the outside with silver foil paper, allowing a little extra at the top to turn over and glue. (This will be easier if you snip down to the tin.) Decorate it with strips of ribbon.

2 Take a block of florist's foam and cut it to fit inside the tin, using the extra pieces to fill in any gaps around the sides.

3 Now wire up pieces of gift wrap ribbon, little baubles, strips of crêpe paper and silk flowers. Curl the ribbon by running the blunt edge of a pair of scissors along it. Push the wires into the foam, arranging them until the tin is totally full. Use strips of ribbon around the outside, and let them fall over the side of the tin.

Holiday Centrepiece

A BOWLFUL OF STREAMERS
AND BAUBLES MAKES A
JOLLY CENTREPIECE

1 To make clusters of small baubles, first remove the hanging strings from the baubles. Put a dab of glue inside the neck of each bauble and push in a short length of florist's wire. Leave them to dry.

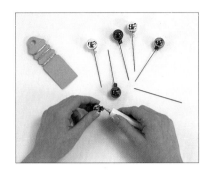

2 Hold the wired baubles in a cluster and wind fine fuse wire or florist's wire around the stems to hold them together.

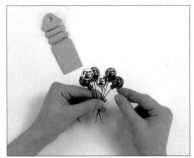

3 Wrap a piece of shiny gift wrap ribbon around the stems and tie it into a bow. Arrange the bauble clusters along with some large glass baubles, feathers and other ornaments in a glass bowl as shown.

Fashion Flowers

MAKE THIS FUN FLORAL
CENTREPIECE OUT OF
NYLON STOCKINGS

1 To make the flowers, first cut some pieces of copper wire 8in (20cm) long. Bend each into a petal shape with pliers. You need five petals for each flower. Cut the nylons into pieces and stretch them over the wire very tightly, binding them at the base with green tape.

2 Next take five stamens (obtainable from craft shops), bend them in half and use pliers to attach them to the end of a long piece of copper wire, again binding them with green tape.

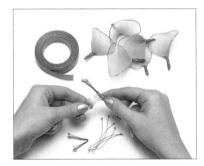

3 Now arrange the petals around the stamens. Start by placing the middle two opposite each other. Bind them, then add the other three around them. When all the petals are in place, tape around the top of the 'stem' and continue down it to the end. When you have made several blooms, wrap them in shiny paper and tie a net bow around the outside.

Fantastic

DECORATE THE TABLECLOTH
OR WALL WITH PRETTY
NET FANS

1 The fans are made from strips of net about 12in (30cm) wide and 40in (1 metre) long. Cut two strips of each colour and fold them crosswise concertina-style, creating the two layers as one. When you have finished pleating, make a few stitches through the net at one end to hold it together.

2 Sew little pearl beads or silver sequins on to the net to decorate it. Trim away any rough edges on the outside of the fan.

3 Finish off by spraying some round wooden beads with silver paint and sewing them to the centre of the fan to cover the pleating.

Pretend Balloons

DECORATE THE WALLS WITH
THESE UNBURSTABLE
FUN BALLOONS

1 Cut out several balloon shapes from coloured cardboard or stiff paper, then cover them on one side with spray-on glitter.

2 Two balloon shapes can be glued together at the edges, or they can all be strung up separately. Tape the balloons to a length of colourful striped ribbon.

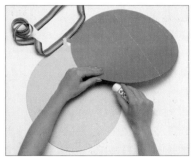

3 Lastly, use more of the same ribbon to make up some bows, and fix them to the balloons with some double-sided tape.

Happy Halloween

CELEBRATE HALLOWEEN YEAR
AFTER YEAR WITH THIS
COLOURFUL PUMPKIN

1 Cut out two satin shapes, following the general outline shown opposite. Place the right sides together and sew around the edge, leaving the flat part at the bottom open. Turn the shape the right side out, slip in a piece of medium-weight wadding (batting), and slipstitch the gap closed.

2 Mark the quilting lines with tacking (basting) stitches using dark thread. Now machine quilt, using a small zig-zag stitch and orange thread. If you haven't got a machine, a small backstitch will be fine. Remove the tacking when you have finished.

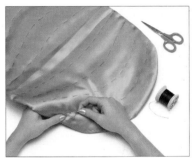

3 Cut out the eyes, mouth and stem in black and green felt. The loop is another piece of felt, about 5in (13cm) long, which you can sew under the edge of the stem. Sew the felt pieces on with a machine satin stitch using orange thread.

Wedding Bells

WELCOME THE BRIDE AND
GROOM WITH THESE
FINE SILVER BELLS

1 First cut out two bell shapes from plain cardboard, following the general outline shown here. Peel the backing off some silver sticky-backed plastic and place the cut-outs on top, pressing firmly. Then cut around the bell shapes.

2 Glue the loops at the top of the bells together, spreading the bell shapes apart as shown.

3 Curl some gift wrap ribbon by running the blunt edge of a scissor blade along it; attach the ribbon to the bells. Finish off with a bow tied through the loops and some tiny birds cut from foil paper.

Birds on the Wing

A CHEERFUL MOBILE MAKES
A PERFECT DECORATION
FOR ANY HOLIDAY

1 The mobile is made from cardboard bird shapes with fanned tissue paper wings and tails. For each bird cut two bird shapes. Glue the two pieces together, placing thread between them, in line with the wings, by which to hang the bird. Cut a slit in the body for the wings.

2 To make the fanned wings, take a piece of tissue paper 14 by 9in (35 by 22cm) and concertina-fold it lengthwise. Round off the edges and push the folded paper through the slit in the bird, so that there is an equal amount on each side. Glue the inside edges upward to the sides of the bird to make the wings fan out.

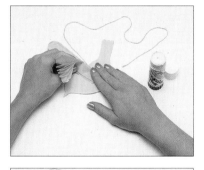

3 For the tail use a piece of tissue paper 14 by 5in (35 by 12cm) and concertina-fold it widthwise. Round off the edges, then slip one end over the tail of the cardboard bird; glue it in place as shown. Glue on sequins for the eyes. Hang the birds from two crossed sticks, tied or glued together, and add gift wrap ribbon curls for the finishing touch.

Window Wonders

BRIGHTEN UP A GLOOMY DAY
WITH THESE 'STAINED
GLASS WINDOWS'

1 These designs are cut from black art paper and backed with coloured tissue. First cut pieces of art paper 15 by 12in (38 by 30cm). Mark a 1in (2.5cm) border all the way around. Now draw your design, taking care that it is always connected in some way to the outer border.

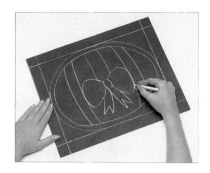

2 Next cut away any parts of the picture that you want to be coloured, taking care not to detach the black areas from the frame.

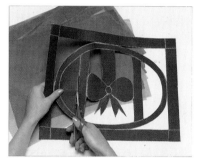

3 Now glue tissue paper to the back. For your first attempt use just one colour; then as you feel more confident, you can build up pictures using three or more different coloured tissues. When the picture is finished, affix it lightly to the window pane, then watch what happens when the light shines through it.

Jack-o'-Lantern

FRIGHTEN AWAY THE SPOOKS
THIS HALLOWEEN WITH A
PUMPKIN LANTERN

1 First take a ripe pumpkin and cut a slice off the top. Scoop out the insides, leaving a good ½ to 1in (1 to 2.5cm) rind. Use the flesh to make a pumpkin pie. The seeds can also be eaten. Wash and dry them, then place them on a baking tray and sprinkle them with salt. Bake them in the oven until they are dry and crunchy.

2 Now mark the eyes, nose and mouth on the front of the pumpkin with a black felt pen. Add a couple of teeth to give the face more character.

3 Cut carefully around the lines, and then push the features out from the inside. Rinse out the inside of the pumpkin, and dry it thoroughly with paper towels. Finally, pop a couple of night lights or small candles inside and light them. Put the top on the pumpkin and place the Jack o'-lantern on a window sill.

Harlequin Masks

IT'S PARTY TIME SO ADD A
TOUCH OF INTRIGUE WITH
A SPARKLING MASK

44

1 You can buy ready-moulded masks from a stationer's or toy shop. The half-mask shown here is coloured with stencil crayons. Starting with pink, apply a little colour to a piece of waxed paper, then pick it up on a stencil brush. Using a circular motion, cover about half the mask. Repeat with the blue, filling in the gaps and giving the eyes a semblance of eyeliner.

2 Next take a short length of lace and glue it to the back of the top half of the mask. Glue some strands of curling gift wrap ribbon on either side. (Curl the ribbon by running the blunt edge of a pair of scissors along it.) Lastly, glue some large sequins over the tops of the ribbons to hide the ends, and glue another one in the centre of the forehead.

3 For the black mask, first sew some silver tinsel wire around the edge and around the eyes. Sew on some pearl beads either side, then sew two or three grey or white feathers under the edges for an owlish look.